THE BOY ON THE ROOF:

and other poems

BY KELLY ROSE

©2019

The boy on the roof: and other poems by Kelly Rose

Author's note: Some of these poems are loosely based on personal experiences. Others, however, are complete fabrications. They are inspired by the images used for the book.

THE WOLF

My daughter is missing
My heart pounds in my chest, terrified that something has happened to her
These woods are not a place for a six-year-old to walk around on their own
There are bears out here, wolves
The woods go on for miles and miles
There are many local stories about hikers who leave the path, never to be heard from again
Cora is not safe out there
The woods are dark, foreboding
I run along the path, looking for any sign of her
Branches gnarled and twisted, reaching out to snag on my clothes

They are like witch's fingers, trying to grab and pull me deeper into the woods

I have been walking for ages, through dense forest that seems to stretch on for eternity

"Where are you?" I call out, hoping desperately for an answer.

Cora has been missing for so long. I fear I may never find her

We had slipped into the woods to escape for a while, to find solace among the evergreens

I had had a long day at work, and when I had picked Cora up from school, she'd said that she'd had a bad day at school as well

Some days are like that. Bad all over.

I had suggested we go out for ice cream, just Cora and I.

We'd been driving home, when Cora had seen the sign for the walking trails

She'd asked if we could go for a walk in the deep, dark woods

I had whole-heartedly agreed

I'd made a game of it, pointing out the different types of trees, the different kinds of birds

Cora had seemed happier for a while

When she disappeared, I thought she were playing a game at first

I expected her to jump out from behind a tree, to shout *boo*, and burst into peals of laughter

But Cora were gone. Footprints leading away in the soft soil, and then *nothing*.

No trace of her, where she'd gone

I look around, trying to get my bearings.

The path is long, winding around the thick-trunked trees

I have walked along the main path, and the smaller ones

Still, I have not found my daughter.

Panic begins to set in

That tree looks familiar

I think I must've passed it twice already.

Yes, I'm sure of it!

Oh, God. I'm going in circles

The sun has already begun to set

The trees are so tall, so dense

I can only see glimpses of sunlight peering through the stately branches above me

Soon, I will be thrust into inky darkness, forced to stumble through the woods while I try to find my daughter

Up ahead, I see a flash of colour among the trees

Bright yellow, like sunflowers

My heart skips a beat

I know it's Cora – she was wearing her knitted yellow hoody when she disappeared

"Cora!" I call out, rushing forward. "Hey! Stop running!"

I run as fast as I can in the darkening woods, nearly tripping on the rutted tree roots

To my left, I hear a howl

A wolf!

I run faster, branches scratching at my face, my hands

I stumble, nearly fall to my hands and knees

And then, I am standing on the edge of a clearing.

Cora has stopped running.

She's standing as still as a statue, her hands clenched at her sides

She is staring straight ahead, her eyes wide

I frown, wondering what she is seeing, what's scared her so bad

And then I see it – *the wolf.*

It steps out of the woods, eyes fixed on my daughter

The wolf pads toward her, his paws silent on the grass

My daughter doesn't move, is frozen in place

I can't allow the wolf to get her

My heart pounds, as I reach down and pick up a rock

My eyes never leave the wolf, watching as it advances slowly towards her

The wolf lets out a low growl

"Mommy, I'm scared!" Cora cries out. She has begun to cry.

"Cora," I say, slowly walking towards her. "I need you to stay calm."

I step in front of her, a human shield

When I am close enough, I throw the rock as hard as I can at the wolf

It hits him square in the shoulder

The wolf yips, lets out a sharp cry

I bend down, pick up another rock.

The wolf has dragged his attention from my daughter, to me.

He is so beautiful, so threatening.

I have never seen a wolf up close like this. From a distance, yes. But he is right in front of me!

I throw the rock, my aim true.

The rock glances off the wolf's leg

He takes a step back, shaking his head from side to side

I fear suddenly, that the wolf will rise quick to anger, rush at me, at Cora.

He could tear us to shreds, rip our throats out, tear flesh from bone.

I stare the wolf down.

"Get away from us!" I shout at the wolf, taking a step forward. I puff out my chest, trying to look bigger, more menacing.

There is no way I'm letting this creature go after me, or my daughter.

It is a long moment, as we stare each other down.

His ears twitch occasionally, eyes narrowing.

And then, the wolf turns around and walks slowly back into the woods

I run to my daughter, kneel in front of her.

I wrap my arms around her, pulling her into a tight embrace

"Are you okay? I was so worried!" I murmur, pressing my face against her scratchy, woolen sweater. "Cora, you scared me."

"I got lost!" Cora tells me. "I couldn't find you!"

I check her over, make sure she's okay

She has a few scratches, but she's alright

I stand up, take her hand.

We start to walk through the woods, back to the trail
It will lead us through the dense forest, guide us back home
All that matters, is that Cora is safe.

THANKFUL FOR YOU

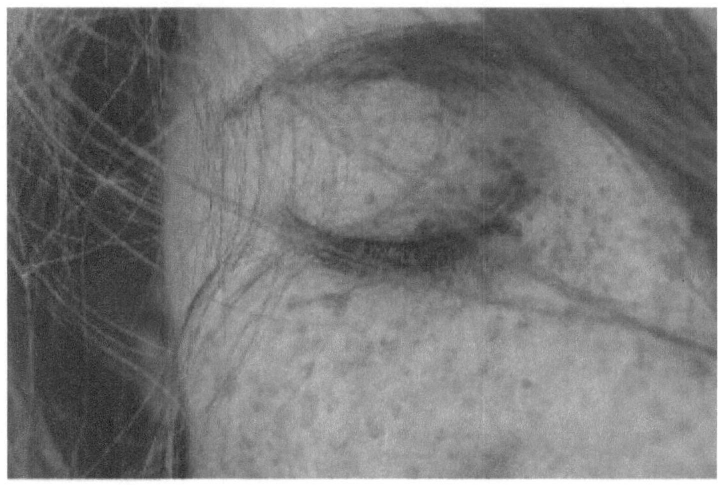

We're standing on the bridge, staring down at the grey river water
You're holding the black umbrella over our heads, keeping us dry
I'm glad you've remembered the umbrella – I'm always so forgetful. I
always leave it behind
I brush your hair out of your eyes, and kiss you
Freckles dot your face, light brown flecks dotting your skin
You are sun-kissed and beautiful
It has been raining so much this week; the water rises, swelling
It rushes below our feet, roaring wildly like a stampede of wild horses
The cars rush past us, high beams cutting through the fog, the heavy rain
The cars drive through the puddles
Frigid water splashes against our sneakers, our jeans
All I can look at, is you.
Your vibrant red hair moves in the brisk wind, getting into your eyes
I reach down, and grab a handful of small pebbles

I fling them into the swollen river, one after another.

They don't even make a ripple. The river swallows them up.

My feet ache in my cheap sneakers, my chest tight from breathing in the cold autumn air

Winter is fast approaching, the air has a sharp bite

We've been walking for hours, down busy sidewalks, past store windows decorated with turkeys and autumn leaves

The thanksgiving decorations are bright, and cheerful – a stark contrast from the gunpowder skies, and the driving rain

All over the city, families and friends are gathering, spending time together in the colder weather

I have so much to be thankful for.

I am alive, in good health

My job is going well enough. Maybe I'll get a promotion one of these days

We can certainly use the money

I am most thankful for you, my ginger goddess

The day I married you, was the happiest day of my life

Our white wedding gowns were white and lacy, long-sleeved, and layers of material

Wife, and wife.

I kissed you so passionately when the pastor said those beautiful words.

It's been nearly a year, since we married. It's almost our anniversary.

I hadn't imagined that this what we'd be doing for our first thanksgiving as a couple

And yet, here we are.

Standing on the bridge, the cold raindrops falling on us, down our faces like cold tears

I am not sad, though. How can I be? You're here, by my side.

We don't have a family to go to, a big turkey with pumpkin pie, and a table laden with side dishes

My parents have passed on, and you don't talk to yours anymore.

We make our own family.
We don't have the warm atmosphere, with cousins, and uncles, siblings, and parents all sitting around the table
But what we do have, is us. And that's enough.
This year, we are going to the thanksgiving dinner downtown at the soup kitchen
It's a long walk, but I'm okay with that.
I'd walk to the ends of the earth for you.
I'm glad you're here with me, by my side
We'll go in, stand in line with the other hundreds of people, some homeless, some down on their luck
Money is tight for us this year. We are barely scraping by.
We'll get two plates of turkey dinner, and two Styrofoam cups of coffee, and grab our seats at one of the long folding tables
We'll eat, spooning some gravy, and cranberry sauce on our plate
Maybe they'll have a basket of dinner rolls, and those little butter packets
My mouth waters at the very idea of it, my empty stomach rumbles
I've been to the soup kitchen dinners in the past, when I was a young child
My dad had been unemployed for a time
I sat at the long table, perched on the fold-out chair between my parents
I was too short to reach the floor, my feet swinging as I nibbled on the dinner roll
I expect it will be much like that
I feel your eyes on me
You're studying me, with your pale green eyes. You smile.
I know it's time to move on, to keep walking
If we get there too late, we might not get any food
"Come on," I say, linking my arm in hers. "Let's go."
We continue walking, her holding the umbrella over both of our heads to keep us dry.

Next year, I promise, we'll scrape enough money together to make our own thanksgiving dinner
We'll get a turkey, or maybe a little chicken, and we'll cook up all kinds of root vegetables
We'll get pecan pie, and whipped cream
And I'll make my mom's cranberry sauce recipe, a whole batch of it
Maybe we'll even buy a nice bottle of wine
I swear, I'll do anything for you
Every day, I am eternally thankful to have you in my life
I am thankful for your patience, your never-ending love
I am thankful that you've stood by with me, through the good times and the bad
You, my amazing wife, make me try harder to be a better person.
Even when we have to walk halfway across the city in the torrential rain, you have never complained. Not even once.
Our first thanksgiving may not have gone as planned, but that's okay.
We have dozens of thanksgivings to make up for it.

THE WITCH

Our new house sits on the top of the hill, nestled in the forty acres of dense woods

We've moved here from the city

We have a stable, with horses

Mom is happy with the move – there is enough land to grow vegetables, and sunflowers

We have lived here for a few weeks

My brother, Peter, insists that the woods are haunted.

He tells everyone he meets about the witch who lives in the woods

Peter says that he met her on the first day we moved in.

She has thick black hair covering most of her face, and lives in a little hut in the woods

Peter said the witch chased after him, and that he'd seen her up near the house a few times

I don't believe him. Witches aren't real.
I think he's just been watching too many scary movies
Every time there's a knock on the door, or a loud noise in the woods,
Peter gets really scared
He keeps telling us that the witch is trying to get him
Tonight, it is raining out.
We are curled up in front of the TV, watching a movie with our parents
Peter keeps pestering mom and dad about the witch.
He wants to know where she came from, how to stop her
He wants to know what kind of weapon he can use to kill the witch
There is a loud howling sound outside
Peter grabs Mom's hand, scared that the witch is outside
She shushes him, says it's just the wind
Suddenly, the power goes out.
We are plunged into darkness. Peter and I scream in terror.
I hear the front door bang open, and a gust of wind rushes in
The room suddenly smells rank, like sulphur, and rotting meat
I put my hand over my nose, trying to find my family in the dark
My fingers brush against somebody, and I grab their hand
"Mom?" I ask.
I recoil. Their hand feels nothing like my mother's – it is dry, and wrinkled, and papery
It feels like an old person's hand.
I reach out, and grasp something soft, my fingers entwined in a thin material
I rip away a handful of cloth, clutching it in my fist
The lights go on again.
Once my eyes adjust, I realize that Peter and I are alone in the living room
"Mom?" I call out. "Dad?"
There are large wet footprints leading to and from the open front door
Our parents are gone.

"The witch took them!" Peter yelled. "She took mom and dad! She's going to eat them!"
I try to reason with him, console him
It couldn't have been the witch. They don't exist
I'm sure our parents are fine
Peter is having none of it. He is convinced of their fate
It's been an hour. Our parents are still gone
The wind continues to howl, rain lashing at the window
I begin to wonder if there is any merit to Peter's story
Is there really a witch that lives in our woods?
I look at the material in my hand, filthy black cloth torn away from whoever had stood beside me in the dark
I hold it up for Peter to see.
"I think you're right," I say. "The witch was here."
At dawn, we go out into the woods
We are on a rescue mission, to bring back our parents
We arm ourselves, bringing the baseball bat, and Peter's slingshot
I don't know the way to the witch's house – I am glad that Peter has already been there before
He leads the way
He marches alongside me, expression hardened
Fiercely determined
We walk through the woods, side-by-side
We talk about our plans for taking down the witch
Peter wants to kill the witch. He wants to make her pay for taking our parents, for scaring him that day in the woods
He even jokes about throwing her in the oven, Hansel-and-Gretel style
I don't want to kill her
All I want to do, is take my parents home
The witch can live in the woods, as long as she doesn't hurt us again
I'm not a killer
Soon, we have reached the witch's house

Peter points it out – it is a tiny stone house, with a thick wooden door
It is very small, probably only one or two rooms
It is a very well-maintained property, with a garden, and a little well
There is a plume of grey smoke rising from the chimney
Someone is home.
Peter and I march up to the door, and I bang my fist on the door
I hear muttering behind the door, the sound of low voices
"Hey, witch!" I call out. "Give me back my parents!"
The witch opens the door, towering over us
Her black hair is long, obscuring most of her face
She crooks her gnarled finger, gesturing us to come closer
I look past her to see my parents
They are sitting at the table, hands tied to the chair armrests
"Give them back!" I shout, enraged.
The witch barely glances at me, even as I dart past her
I rush to my father's side, and tug at the rope restraints
They are knotted so tightly, there is no way that I can possibly break them free
The witch is staring at Peter
"I will give them back, once you return what is mine."
I frown, looking from the witch, to Peter
Peter is shaking, terrified
He looks close to tears
The witch stares at Peter, and repeats her demand
"Peter?" I ask, going to him
He looks so small, so frail
Peter reaches into his pocket, and pulls something out of his front pocket
He holds his fist out to the witch, then opens his hand
A tiny golden orb rests on his palm, shimmery and bright
The witch shakes her long hair out of her eyes, and smiles
She reaches out, tentatively takes the golden orb from Peter's hand
The witch examines it, turning it slowly

She nods, satisfied

"What is it?" I ask, mesmerised by the gleaming object in her hand

It is so pretty.

"My magic," the witch says, her voice low. "My magic comes from this orb."

She explains that the orb fell out of her necklace when she was out for a walk

Peter found it, kept it

She kidnapped our parents to use as leverage, until Peter would finally return what was rightfully hers

Without her magic, the witch was withering away

She used the last of her magic to transport our parents to her cabin during the storm

It was a last-ditch effort

Once she was done explaining, the witch sets the orb back into her necklace

It glows brightly, then dims back to its original colour

I quickly set the baseball bat down, and untie my parents

The knots are easy to undo, now

"I'm sorry I stole your magic!" Peter calls out, still fearful

The witch smiles. Her face is no longer lined with age, no longer terrifying in its ghastly appearance

She looks younger, rejuvenated

I realize that she is around mom's age, give or take a few years

"I forgive you, Peter," the witch said. "I scared you that day, in the woods. I didn't mean to."

We go back home

After that, things are calm

My mother befriends the witch, invites her over for tea once a week to catch up

And my brother is no longer scared of the witch, or the woods

We are neighbourly towards her

DROWNING

Sometimes, I feel like I'm drowning

As a child, things seemed simpler

I focused on schoolwork, played with my friends until the streetlights came on, I spent my allowance on candy

Each year, it seems there is so much more to bog me down

Cement blocks tied to my feet

Adult responsibility – things like mortgage, soaring food prices, and failing relationships – anchor me to the lake floor

I expend all my energy, fighting desperately, until my limbs ache from exhaustion

Every year I get older, sicker

Relationships crumble, friendships grow distant and eventually dissolve

People pass on – family, friends, acquaintances

Grief and loss weighs me down, until I feel like I can't push myself to the surface

My lungs are oxygen-starved, and though I can see the surface, I can't rise up enough to suck in a mouthful of air
It takes every ounce of determination and grit to break the surface
I breathe in the sweet oxygen, blinking in the sunlight
And I look around, realizing that I'm not the only one struggling
The whole lake is full of people suffering, trying to stay afloat
We struggle to keep our heads above water, despite our struggles and circumstances
Some of us will be caught in a never-ending struggle of drowning, rising to the surface
Some will fight desperately, but end up losing. They will finally open their mouths, and it will fill with water
And some of us manage to stay above the water, and stay afloat
The ones who make it, who stay afloat – they can reach in a helping hand and pull out the ones who still are drowning below the surface
Life can be quite stressful at times, but always remember – you don't have to drown in silence
It's okay to ask for help

CLOCKWORK GIRL

Clockwork girl, I love you so
You're lying there, eyes closed
These past few days, you were slowing down
Body creaking, grating metal-on-metal sound
I took you to the scientists, begged that they repair you
It cost so much, but I don't care
I'd sell our house to pay for your upgrades
I'd sell my kidney to fix you
God, I can never get used to seeing you like this
I'm glad you are asleep
They've removed your chest plate, clockwork innards carefully pulled out
piece-by-piece
This is what you've been reduced to – pieces of metal, tubes, and gears
It's unnatural, that you're still alive
The worst day of my life, was when you died

I was the one that found your lifeless body
I picked you up, cradled you in my arms
You were my miracle baby – after years of trying, I was finally able to conceive
I couldn't bear the thought of losing you soon
They were able to fix you, make things right again
You will need constant check-ups, constant upgrades
If I don't maintain your upgrades, your body will eventually fail
It is worth every penny
Although you now are constructed of flesh, and machinery, you are still my beloved daughter
This is the only way I can keep you just a little bit longer
I can see you play outside with your friends
I can curl up in bed with you, read to you
I'll see you graduate from school
Maybe I can even walk down the aisle
I know you don't always understand my reasons behind turning you into a clockwork girl
I believe wholeheartedly that it was the best decision I ever made for you

THE PROPOSAL

The driver ahead of us skids on a patch of black ice, nearly hitting the guard rail
Ice pellets hit the windshield, sharp and aggressive
Plink! Plink!
I worry one of them might crack the windshield, worry that we might go off the road from the ice
I glance over at Jennifer, the concern showing on my face
She smiles, glancing briefly at me
"You good?" Jennifer asks, her fingers drumming on the steering wheel along with the weak radio signal
I nod.
Two more hours, and then we'll be there

I'm nervous as hell, a cold sweat dripping down my spine despite the heat pouring out of the registers

I pull down the mirror, and run my fingers through my hair

"You look fine, Babe," Jennifer tells me, reaching out to grasp my hand.

She kisses me on the knuckles, her eyes still on the road

We've been dating for six months

God, was it only six months?

It feels like longer

I feel like I can divide my entire life into two categories – before I met Jennifer, and afterwards

We met during an art show for our school

Our art college is small, and surprisingly, we had never crossed paths before that day

Jennifer does oil paintings, I sculpt

I love Jennifer with my whole heart. She's absolutely amazing

Where would I be without her? She's my everything.

"Are you sure your parents will like me?" I ask. "Are you sure they're okay with me coming to your family dinner?"

Every time I ask, she says yes. Of course they'll like me. And of course I'm good to come for dinner.

Still, I need affirmation

Meeting the girlfriend's parents for the first time is nerve-wracking

It'd be stressful enough for a regular dinner with her folks, but this was Christmas dinner

That was some high expectations

I'd be meeting aunts, uncles, cousins, nephews – the whole family

She tells me about her family, about how her mother is Jewish, and her father is Presbyterian

They celebrate both Hanukkah, and Christmas – and invite family from both sides

None of them know that we've been dating

Jennifer wants to break the news in person

She says her parents will love me
She says they're great people.
They know she's bringing a friend from college, but that's all
I wanted to fly over, since they lived so far away
Jennifer said it'd be better if we drove.
She likes road trips, likes the passing scenery
Besides, Jennifer reasons, it'd cost too much for us to get a flight this close
to Christmas
And there's this snowstorm to contend with
We have limited visibility from the ice fog, the blowing snow
We loaded up the vehicle with wrapped presents for her family, and our
luggage, and we hit the road
It's a two-day drive
It's been a long drive, but not unbearably so
Soon, the snow-covered fields gave way to hills
Now, there are huge snow-capped mountains
I have never seen anything like it
They are majestic, rising high up into the sky
My ears pop as we slowly drive up the mountain
The road is small and winding, sheer cliffs a few feet from us, giving way
to valleys and rivers far below us
I'm scared to look down
I've always lived on the flat prairies, used to the earth stretching out for
miles
We stop a few times on the way, eating at diners, and truck stops
We sleep in a motel with ugly floral bedding, and watch 'A Christmas
Story' on cable
It's been a good trip
I flip through the radio stations, but I can't find anything good
The mountains are blocking the radio waves
Soon, we have reached her parent's house
It is a stately brick house, with white pillars on the front

It's decorated with hundreds of white and blue Christmas lights, boughs of holly and ivy in the windows, and a large wreath on the door

They have a ten-foot tree in the front room, presents stacked up under the perfectly arranged decorations

I give a low whistle

"This is where you grew up?" I ask, impressed.

Jennifer nods

I knew she was well off, but I didn't realize she lived in such a rich neighbourhood.

Everything is *perfect*. Too perfect.

We pull into the long driveway, parking behind the other cars

We grab our bags, and go to the front door

"Jennifer!" her mom exclaims, pulling open the front door. "I'm so glad you're here! We were beginning to worry!"

She is a short woman, unnaturally skinny. She has a wide smile, friendly enough.

Jennifer introduces us, and I shake hands with her mother.

Her hair is peroxide blonde, clashing against her beige and white sweater, and her chunky necklaces

As we venture further into the house, we are bombarded with family members

I don't know how I'll keep everyone's names in my head; there's just too many of them

We hand out presents.

Her nieces and nephews rip into the Christmas presents, excitedly showing off their new presents

We went all out on the gifts, needing to impress them

Jennifer hasn't spent the holidays with them for a few years, since she lives so far away

Dinner begins shortly, and we all sit around the large table

There seems to be never-ending dishes to try

Turkeys and hams, mashed potatoes, turnips, four types of stuffing

Not to mention the pies!

The food is eaten, crackers ripped open

Everyone is drinking wine, and eggnog

"Guys, I have an announcement to make," Jennifer says, standing up. "I'd like everyone's attention, please."

Every looks up at her, giving her a curious look

We're all wearing those funny paper crowns that we pulled out of our Christmas crackers

We've all read our corny jokes out loud, most of them barely funny

Some of the kids are playing with their new trinkets from the holiday crackers – dreidels, and cheap plastic rings, whistles, and toy animals

"By now I presume you have all met my friend from college, Erica. We've been dating for six months."

I take a few sips of ice-cold water, my heart fluttering

Her aunts and uncles are giving me curious looks, her father simply raises his eyebrows at his daughter.

"Erica, I have something to ask you."

Jennifer takes out a ring from her front pocket, and turns to me. "Erica, would you do the honour of being my wife?"

There is an audible gasp from her aunts and uncles, and they all stare at us with surprise

Her mother is standing in the doorway, sipping a large glass of peach wine

Her eyes wide with shock

She's not the only one in shock

Six months. We've been together for such a long time.

And we have never talked about getting married

I'm shocked that she's proposing to me.

And to do it so publicly? In front of her whole family?

I blink rapidly, suddenly fearful that they will not take her engagement announcement well

I don't know these people

I don't know if they're okay with gay marriage

They could be – god forbid – *republican*.

Before today, her family wasn't even aware that Jennifer was a lesbian.

They'd had no idea that she'd been dating me for the past six months.

I wish Jennifer had proposed to me in private, not in front of her entire family

I don't know them, don't know how they'll react to her coming out like this.

I realize that I haven't answered her question

Jennifer is staring at me expectantly

The silence in the room drags on

I stand up, and Jennifer puts a reassuring hand on my shoulder

"I would love to be your wife, Jennifer," I say, my voice a little shaky. "I accept."

The room breaks out into a babble of conversation

Jennifer's mom is the first to congratulate us

She rushes forward, her arms opening wide to envelop her daughter

"Oh, I'm so happy for you!" she proclaims, pulling me into a hug. "You're going to be my daughter-in-law, Erica! This is fantastic!"

And just like that, it's okay.

Her family members congratulate us, hand shaking, and hugging

I am awash with relief, glad to included into her family like this

Jennifer and I, we're getting married

I think a summer wedding would be nice. I've always fancied marrying outdoors, maybe in a field somewhere

Jennifer wants to marry in the synagogue, the same one her parents married in

We have a lot of details to work out

But that's okay – we have months to prepare for the big day

I can't wait to call her my wife.

MIDSUMMER

Elin stands on the beach, staring at the white-capped cresting waves
The air is thick with brine, the sweet perfume of the sea
She has woven a rainbow of flowers into a crown, set it comfortably on her crown
It is Midsummer's day, the summer solstice
The day has been long, full of festivities
It is evening now, though it's hard to tell the hour
The midnight sun still shines brightly, as bright now as it was at the start of the festivities
Most everyone is still at the festival, drinking and singing
Their singing carries on the wind
Elin has slipped away for a while, needing to be alone with her thoughts

She finds the beach sounds comforting, the best music one could ever ask for
Everyone is eating herring, as it is the main food staple of the festival
Pickled herring, or wrapped in foil with butter and asparagus, broiled, and layered herring
She likes hers wrapped in foil, cooked with butter and dill, with roasted carrots and asparagus
She stands, silently listening to the seagulls above, and the waves
Distantly, she can still hear the revelers singing, laughing raucously as they chug their beers
Children run around, weaving in between the cluster of adults
Midsummer is the best time of year
It is when the days are the longest, the sun shining brightly – high into the sky
Winter is too cold, too dark
It is the sort of dark that seems to never end, the coal-black darkness of outer space
It's dreary, and lonely – half of the year spent in utter darkness
But midsummer is much better than all that dark, and bone-chilling cold
Midsummer is light, and fertility, happiness, and abundance
Elin has gone to the festival every year
When she was little, her favourite part used to be dancing around the maypole
She used to love getting all dressed up in traditional garb, dancing in sync with the other young people of her town
They would wind the ribbons around and around the pole, colours braiding together in a gorgeous rainbow
Elin hasn't done any of that for a few years
Now that she is a bit older, her favourite part has become dancing around the bonfire
Elin starts to walk back to the festival
They are already lighting the bonfire

She smiles, softly cutting through the tall grass at the edge of the clearing
A few people smile, wave at her
No longer having to dance in sync with the other children at the maypole, she finds that the bonfire dancing is a much more freeing sort of thing
Arms moving wildly, veins full of drink, Elin loves to dance alongside her friends and neighbours
Sparks fly up into the smoky air
The logs crackle, fire spits and pops
The fire licks hungrily at the sky, always reaching, striving for more
Its appetite is never sated
There is a wildness, a sense of liberty
Elin is soon joined by others, as the fire continually burns
There is a sense of community, of togetherness
She holds hands with her neighbour, and her younger sister, and they dance around the fire
Everyone is in a broad circle, constantly moving
There are no staunch rules, no demands or expectations
Every time she dances at the bonfire, she is reminded of the festival's pagan roots
Elin feels connected to her witch ancestors, to all the people who branch out in her large family tree
Her grandmother and mother have taken Elin to every midsummer festival since her birth
And when she has a daughter, she will take her annually as well

ARTIST'S MUSE

He says I am his muse
He says that every time he sees me, he is drawn by my beauty
I inspire him
Every time we are together, he is struck with the greatest of inspiration
I have lost track of how many times he has painted, or sketched me
It must be in the thousands
I pose for him, sitting on the stool in the centre of his art studio
He instructs me how to hold my arms, where to place my legs so as to fulfil his vision
I can hold myself in position for ever so long now

I pride myself in being his subject
My hands are delicately pointed, wrists bent at slight angles
Sometimes I am fully clothed, sometimes I am bare
He asks me to sit at his reading bench at the window, posing with a copy
of Jane Eyre, or Hunchback of Notre Dame
He likes the natural light seeping in from the wide window
Sometimes he sketches me doing regular, mundane things – eating toast,
or playing the piano
He says I am beautiful no matter what I'm doing
He has a full wardrobe of clothes in my studio – roaring twenties flapper
dresses, tuxedoes, cloaks, and bonnets
I wear whatever he tells me to, pretending to be people from all sorts of
time periods
I wear the various brooches, the necklaces, the silver and gold rings
He has wigs, too
He is such a brilliant artist
I am not his only subject, but I *am* his favourite subject
His paintings hang in museums, they sell in galleries
Sometimes it is a lonely business, being the wife of a painter
Every day, he sits up in his art studio for hours, surrounded by hundreds
of paints, brushes, and canvases
When he closes the door to his studio, I know that he needs to be alone
Sometimes, I don't see him for ages
Sometimes he gets frustrated because he can't get the painting just right
But eventually, it all works itself out
He tries all sorts of different styles, always wanting to better his craft
He uses all sorts of mediums – oil and acrylic, charcoal, spray paint,
watercolour, and even simple ballpoint pen sketches
Every time he creates a new piece, I am amazed by the stunning attention
to detail, the ability to create such a photo-realistic likeness of myself on
the page
I am glad to be his muse

I will sit for him whenever he asks, pose for him however he wants
Each and every artwork he creates, is beautiful in its own right

THE FLOWER STAND

I had been working at the flower stand for two months
Got hired on at the first of summer, working with my uncle and cousin
Five days a week, I sold assorted potted plants off the side of the road
It wasn't a bad job, exactly
After the first week, I found it boring, monotonous
Water the plants, prune them, sell them
The customers come in waves – a half dozen people show up in their cars,
and then none at all
I keep a book behind the counter, and I read when I have the free time
I thought today's shift would be just as boring as the rest
I was mistaken.
It's Friday afternoon, at a quarter to three, and I see your car drive past
It's been an hour since I've had a customer
You've got a pumpkin-coloured car, the colour catching my eye
I watch you drive slowly past

You're singing along to the radio, mouth moving

One arm is casually hanging out the open window

You see the flower stand, your eyes lighting up

I watch as you pull over to the side of the road

You get out, wait for an opening in the traffic

My eyes never leave you

Your hair is braided, nearly to your waist

You run across the street, kicking up little dust clouds with your red ballet flats

I love your outfit

You're wearing a black and white blouse decorated with tiny flowers

Red frilly skirt that fell down past your knees, moving about as you took each calculated step

And then, you are standing in front of me

For a brief and awkward second, I feel like my mouth is not going to work properly

"Hi!" I finally greet you, giving you a lopsided grin - eager to please

You smiled in return, and began quietly perusing the flowers

I watched you read the labels of each type of flower, lined up in clay pots

Our freshest and most fragrant are on full display, the other ones have wilted in the heat and are not as enticing

"Have you decided what to buy?" I asked, trying to strike up a conversation

You smiled at me, as sweet as can be, and points to the pink and white flowers beside the till

"I like these ones," you told me. "I think they will light up my room quite nicely."

I agreed with you. They really were quite beautiful.

"We have cactuses, and succulents, if you're interested," I told you, trying to find a conversation topic.

I hold out one of the succulents. "Easy to care for."

You smiled at me, took the potted plant from my outstretched hand

"It's very cute."
"Yes," I told her. "Very cute."
I wasn't talking about the succulent
You continued to look at all the rest of the stock
When you finally chose all the plants you wanted, I load them up in a
wooden crate
It's quite heavy, but I don't mind
You tell me that you didn't expect to buy so many plants
You don't have a green thumb. But you wanted to cheer up your
apartment
I carry them to your car, and set them carefully on the backseat of the
pumpkin-coloured vehicle
"You work here every day?"
"Monday through Friday," I said, nodding.
"Good. Maybe I'll see you again sometime."
I grinned at the thought of seeing you again
The weekend crawls by *soo slooowly*
All I can think about, is seeing you again
I don't even know your name
My friends can tell something's on my mind
I'm at the bar, distracted
I'm at home, deep in thought
I'm at the store, pondering
You're permanently on my mind.
Monday morning, I get up earlier for work than normal
My uncle and cousin are surprised
They drink their strong coffee, watching as I scarf down my eggs and
bacon
I'm not normally a morning person
When I am done, I load up the truck and drive to the flower stand
You're already parked at the side of the road, two coffees in hand, waiting
I grin at you, set the crate of flowers down

"Hi," you say. "How are you doing, this fine morning? Want a coffee?"
I take one from you, sip it slowly
"Thanks," I told you. "We meet again."
We get to talking, and you tell me about yourself.
You tell me your name is Adelaide. The sweetest name in the world.
You're a paralegal at a firm downtown
You're a year younger than me, and you've moved from Virginia last year
My heart flutters when I'm around you
Your eyes are so delightful, lighting up like tiny embers as I tell you all about the different types of plants we have
You gush about the flowers, are intrigued to learn that I live on the farm with my family
I tell you about my pet goat, Shirley, and how she's always getting into trouble by escaping her pen
I give you flowers a half-price, wholly enamored with you
You come back every day that week.
Finally, on Friday afternoon, I work up the courage to ask you out for drinks
"Oh, Benjamin, I thought you'd never ask," you said, grinning at me. "I'd love to go for drinks!"
You wrote your number down on a slip of paper, and kissed me on the cheek.
"I'll see you at eight."
I get a bit of light ribbing from my cousin after you leave
He says it's hilarious that it took me so long to ask Adelaide out
I count my lucky stars that I ever met you
I have a date with the prettiest girl in the whole world

MONSTER

George slammed the bathroom door behind him, flipping the lock
The music was pounding, felt the vibrations strongly in his ribcage
He's had too much alcohol, his stomach queasy
He inwardly berated himself for coming tonight
What had he been thinking?
He hadn't known that Thomas would be at the party
He hadn't set eyes on his former partner in two years – not since the night they'd broken up
There was a bitter acrid taste in his mouth, like he might throw up
Thomas, the man who had hurt him so badly
Left him emotionally and physically scarred from their short time together
The scars of their relationship were still present, never fully healing over

It had all started innocuously enough

They'd met at the University library, when George had had an economics paper due

They'd begun casually dating

He'd professed his love to him, told him that they were soul mates

Thomas, with his lovely blond hair, had been so beautiful

George had fallen head-over-heels in love

They'd spent many a night in Thomas' apartment

Thomas had been the first man he'd ever slept with

The man's scent was intoxicating, his words sugary sweet like a Venus fly trap

Luring him in, like he'd done to countless others

Destroying him.

Tonight, seeing him across the room – it had stirred up unwanted memories

Things he had forced down, tried to repress

Like that night, when George had tried to move out

Thomas had blocked his path on the stairwell, cursing at him

He had threatened George, told him if he ever left him, he'd kill him

Thomas had pulled out a handgun from his waistband, pressed the cold metal against George's temple

He'd pulled the trigger, smiled as it clicked

Empty. The gun had been empty.

That didn't make it any less terrifying.

He still woke up in a cold sweat, the click of the gun reverberating through his skull, again and again

He would never get over that night

He hadn't seen or heard form Thomas in two years

It looked like Thomas had found his newest target.

When Thomas had entered the party earlier, he wasn't alone.

There was a younger man with him, their hands entwined

He was young – eighteen, maybe nineteen

Dark hair, tanned skin, pouty lips

George wondered how you two met, what sort of web you spun around him, keeping him as your target

The guy looked at Thomas with such adoration, smiling fondly at him

They looked happy

For a fleeting second, George wondered if maybe his ex had changed

Maybe he was a better person, now.

No. Someone like Thomas couldn't change

He was rotten to the core

George wondered how long they had been dating

Probably not long.

George knew he had to warn the new guy

It never took Thomas long to show his true colours

He could only act like the sweet boyfriend for so long

George splashed water on his face, and stared at his expression

His eyes were haunted, cheeks flushed

He had to step in, stop the cycle

It would be either the smartest thing he had ever done, or the stupidest

Go down there, George told himself. *Go downstairs, and find Thomas' new boyfriend.*

Pull him aside, and tell him what kind of person Thomas really is. Warn him, so he can choose whether to stay or go.

After that, it would be up to the new boyfriend to do what he thought was the right thing.

He needed to make an informed decision

George went downstairs, back into the huge crowd of people

The electronic music blasted away, pulsating beat, and an auto-tuned voice singing about sex and love

George looked around, trying to spot either Thomas or his new partner

The place is packed, the blacklights hurt his eyes

Everyone is dressed up in bright clothes, covered in neon face paint

The music gives George a headache

Finally, he spots Thomas' boyfriend.

He's in the kitchen

The blacklights accentuate his painted face – neon greens and pinks, swirls and triangles

He's refilling his drink, pouring out a generous amount of brandy

"Nice party, eh?" The guy said, nodding at him.

"Yeah," George said. "I'm George."

"Matt."

"You're dating Thomas, right? I saw you two walk in together."

"Yeah!" he said, face lighting up. "Going on two weeks, now. You know him?"

George nodded, a lump in his throat. "Yeah."

He pauses, trying to figure out what to say next

"We dated, actually," George finally said. "Few years back."

Matt frowned, and set the bottle down, recapping it. "Is that so?"

"Yeah. Actually, I was looking for you. There's something you need to know about him."

Matt frowned, studying him. He looked bemused

He sized George up and down, then nodded

"Let's go outside. It's too damned loud in here."

George grabbed a cooler, and followed him of the kitchen

They walked on the dewy grass, drinks in hand

It's quieter out there

The music was muted

George told him how he met Thomas, how they started dating

He told Matt how things were good, for a while

But Thomas had a way of losing his temper over the smallest things - spilled drinks, changed plans, that sort of thing

George recalled how someone had bumped into Thomas at a bar, and it had turned into a violent altercation

The other man needed twenty stiches, and had a concussion

The whole time George talked, Matt was staring at him

Disbelief was clear on his face

He looked confused, upset

"Once he sets his sights on someone," George told him, "Thomas doesn't let them go. He sucks 'em dry, then discards them when he gets bored."

"That doesn't sound like Thomas," Matt said. "I don't believe it."

His face is cold, now. Distant.

He didn't believe him.

George earnestly tried to convince him, tried to get him to listen

Even as Matt started to walk away, George kept talking

"You've got to be careful with someone like him," George said. He grabbed Matt's arm. "He's *toxic*, man."

"Thomas isn't like that!" Matt shouted, pushing him off. "He'd never hurt me. Stop saying this shit! You're just jealous."

George turns around, and froze in his tracks. He dropped the glass bottle in his hand, heard it smash against the ground

Thomas has spotted them.

Thomas marched across the wet grass towards them, a surly expression on his face

The way he moved, it was the stance of a man looking for a fight

Chest puffed out, marching forward, Thomas glared at them

"You!" Thomas shouts out, jabbing a finger against George's chest. "Get away from him!"

George hesitated, then stood his ground. He had begun to shake in fear, but he stayed his ground.

"Thomas – "

"I don't know what this fool is telling you, Matt. None of it is true."

Thomas bent down, picked up the glass bottle

He smashed it against the side of the porch, and held it out

Two men notice what's going on, jump to their feet

George saw them approach

They closed the gap between him, and Thomas. Shouting at them, telling Thomas to drop the bottle.

"You're *dead*, George," Thomas says, the sharp glass glinting in the light.

He rushed forward, lunging at George

George fell to the ground, bleeding from the cuts on his arms

His skin was sliced open, pieces of glass broken off

George screamed out in agony

Thomas crouched above him, pressed the glass against George's face, slashed his cheek

They managed to pull Thomas off of him, grabbed his arms, subdued him

Matt reached down, carefully helps George to his feet

Matt was crying, clutching at him

"Are you okay?" Matt asked, eyes shocky. "I'm sorry – I didn't know he was capable of doing this."

"I'm okay," George murmured quietly.

Blood dripped down his face, down his arms

He was in great pain

Later, the street was covered with flashing reds and blues

George sat in the back of the ambulance, the EMT picking the glass shards out of his arm

Matt broke away from the crowd, walked over to the ambulance

He gave George an apologetic look

"I've pressed charges against him," Matt said. He was still shaking. "Thanks, you know, for warning me. He's a monster."

"Yeah," George said, nodding at him. "I didn't want you getting hurt the way he did to me. And others."

Matt clambers up into the ambulance, and sat down beside George

They watched the EMT clean, and wrap George's cuts

Matt rode with him to the hospital

George tells him that he's glad Matt is safe, relieved that Thomas will be behind bars

Matt stays by his side during his hospital stay

Both of them feel comfortable in each other's presence

Maybe it's the shared trauma bringing them together, or maybe it's the fact that George finds Matt beautiful, and intriguing.

Whatever the reason, they begin dating shortly after.

For all the horrific things that Thomas had done when they had been together, he was inadvertently responsible for George and Matt meeting, and falling in love.

They sure had quite the story to tell their future children.

THE BOY ON THE ROOF

Christopher was a sad, melancholic boy
Even after knowing him for all those years, I know there was still so much of his trauma that I would never be privy to
I had met him when I was eight, nearly nine-year-old
The first time I met him, was up on the roof of my new apartment building
It was a crumbling brick and mortar building – an old warehouse renovated into apartments a few years back
My parents and I moved in on the first of the month, as it was close to my mom's office
Our apartment was nice enough, with new appliances, and lofty ceilings
The place was cold, even in summer

I missed our old place, because it had been near my elementary school, and near all my friends
Now, Mom had to drive me to work in the mornings
The new apartment had an unfriendly air, like we were intruding on someone else's space
Most units were rented out to childless couples, business-types likes my mom
Until I saw Christopher up on the roof, I had been certain that no other children even lived in the building
I thought I was the only one.
My new bedroom was very small, only big enough for my bed, and desk
I had to get rid of some of my books and toys in the move, and the rest were crammed into the tiny bedroom closet
There wasn't really anywhere to play
Dad worked from home, and he always needed plenty of space in the apartment to spread out his work
He needed plenty of quiet to focus on his projects
Mom was always at the office, putting in over-time
The building didn't have a playground on the premises, nor was there a park nearby
I wasn't in school, wasn't at summer camp
I didn't have anywhere to run around and explore, or play on the swings
The doorman frowned upon having me play in the lobby, even if it was a quiet game
He complained to Dad that I was a nuisance, always getting underfoot
I was not to play down there anymore.
And so I took to exploring the old building, learning its nooks and crannies
There was a basement, and a sub-basement – the tenant's storage lockers were padlocked, their contents mysterious and unknown
There were rooms full of breaker panels, and the large furnace that looked like a terrifying beast

It was dark, and clammy – always smelling like mold
I spent some time down there, until I got bored of it
There were multiple staircases, leading all the way up to the top floor
I tried to make a game of them, running up and down the sturdy stairs
Sometimes I'd try to skip steps, seeing how long I could stretch my legs
Sometimes, I'd take my bouncy ball, and bounce it off each step, listening
to the echo in the stairwell
I got in trouble for that game. It was too loud.
But my exploration of the staircases was how I finally found the door
leading to the roof.
It was heavy, a large metal door with a push bar
Two weeks after we'd moved there, I went out onto the roof for the first
time
I squinted in the bright sunlight, my eyes adjusting
The roof of the building had a ledge around the roof, only going up about
three feet
There was a bunch of pigeons cooing and pecking at the roof, grey with
flashes of rainbow on their fat little bodies
A few seagulls and crows perched on the top of the water tower, giving
the occasional caw
It was the first time I met Christopher.
He was standing on the ledge, his back to me
He was a scrawny kid, with thick black hair haloed around his head
I was drawn to him.
I don't know why exactly. Maybe it was because it was the first kid I had
seen in the building, or maybe it was curiosity.
Stretching his thin arms out, black oversized sweatshirt flapped in the
wind like crow's wings
He had tilted his head upwards into the smoggy city air
I walked towards him, trying not to break the silence
It felt like the kind of place where I shouldn't make too much noise
Like in church, where everyone was supposed to stay quiet, somber

It had that kind of feel to it, up on the roof.

The only sound were my faint footsteps, and the cooing of the pigeons

I was nearly at the ledge

I was now close enough to see that his eyes were closed.

I wanted to say something to him, but I didn't know how to find the words

My steps disturbed the flock of pigeons, and they flew up into the air in a flurry of beating wings

The sound of the pigeons startled him, and he turned around, trying to see what had caused their sudden flight

He was so deathly pale. Ghostly pale.

I walked towards him, cautious.

I had reached the ledge, now. Leaned my hip against it.

Had he just been taking in the view? Admiring the brick buildings, and watching the people walk on the sidewalk below?

It was quite a view.

I could see the whole neighbourhood from here, the bridges spanning across the grey river, the light glinting off the skyscrapers downtown

His eyes had been closed, though.

I wondered if he had he been contemplating jumping from the ledge, to his death on the street below?

Oh, god. I hoped not.

The thought scared me. I had never seen anyone die before, except on TV.

I had never seen a dead body, and I certainly didn't want to see one – ever.

That kind of thing would scar me for life.

The boy's body swayed a little, the wind buffeted at his clothes

I imagined for a horrific moment, that the wind would tug at him, pull him over the edge

His arms would pinwheel, trying to grab onto something

And I would be incapable of saving him

I was too short and slim to grab his hand, pull him to safety.

He easily outweighed me; he was a few years older than I.

And he would fall

Down

Down

Down

Until he hit the pavement.

No amount of king's horses could put together a broken egg like that.

Not from this height.

The boy was still staring at me, that startled expression on his face

"No one ever comes up here," the boy said, his voice so soft he was nearly inaudible. "*No one.*"

"Can you come down from there?" I asked, staring up at him.

He nodded, slowly, still staring at me with his haunted eyes

His hands were shaking, body trembling slightly

I reached up my hand to him in offering.

"Come on," I said, nervously. "I'm worried you might fall."

He swiped at his damp eyes, and I wondered if they were like that from the strong winds, or if he had been crying.

For a few seconds, the boy didn't move. I'm not even sure that he heard me

But then he slowly reached down, and grasped my hand. His hand was ice cold.

He lowered himself off the ledge, and stepped back onto the roof

I feel relieved to see him off the ledge

Being up on the ledge like that was dangerous.

The boy sat cross-legged, hands demurely in his lap

I sat down across from him, studying him

His face was thin, angular

It's an unhealthy look, like he missed a few too many meals

He had dark smudges under his slightly sunken eyes

Upturned nose, full lips, eyes so dark I could get lost in them forever

His hair was wild, full of curls and cowlicks, standing up in places where it should be lying flat

He caught my eye, then looked back to the pigeons

At first, neither of us said a word

We just sat, listening to the heavy traffic below, and the pigeons walking around us

I feel comfortable in his presence, glad that he was no longer standing precariously on the narrow ledge

"What's your name?" I asked.

I watched as he pulled a bag out of his jeans pocket, and shook out a portion of its contents into his hand

I realized that it was a bag of dried peas

He began to throw the small green pellets in front of him, one after another

The pigeons swarmed around him, fighting for the food

It was the first time I saw him smile – though it was just the slightest raising of the corner of his mouth

It was barely perceptible

It only lasted a second, and then his face is solemn again

"What's your name?" I asked, curious. "I'm Eden. I've just moved here two weeks ago. I'm in apartment 12 F."

"Christopher."

His voice was soft, lilting.

I held out my hand, and he poured a small amount of dried peas into my palm

We threw them towards the gathering of pigeons, watching them cluster around the food

I wondered if Christopher fed the pigeons every day. Maybe that was why they were so fat.

"Why were up on the ledge?" I asked.

Christopher looked hurriedly away. He had a sad, hang-dog kind of look to him

I didn't know who he was, what he'd been through
But I feel like he'd been through a lot.
Christopher was a few years older than I was - maybe thirteen, or fourteen. He shouldn't have had the weight of the world on his shoulders at that age
"Were you going to jump?" I finally asked. I *needed* to know.
Christopher didn't answer. He was an awfully quiet boy.
Finally, he shrugged.
I wasn't sure if that meant yes, or no.
I stayed with him for the rest of the afternoon
We played a few games, chucking my bouncy ball against the side of the water tower
We drew with colourful chalk on the roof – tic tac toe, and hangman
And we laid in the shade, talking quietly as we listened to the police helicopters flying above the city
I visited him every day.
One day, I brought up my portable DVD player to the roof, and showed him some of my favourite movies
Christopher didn't have a TV at home
He said his Dad didn't like having one in the apartment
We set up my camping tent on the roof, and covered the bottom with pillows, and sleeping bags
A lot of times, we'd stare down at the traffic, the cars and buses as small as little toy cars
He pointed out all the different buildings, told me the history of them.
Christopher knew an awful lot about the neighbourhood, about the people who lived in the area
He watched them so frequently that he knew when they were coming and going
When he got to talking about a topic he liked, Christopher could talk a whole lot
It was nice to hear his voice.

He smiled more frequently, as we got to know each other better
We got to spend quite a lot of time together that summer
I wanted to bring him to my room sometimes, show him all my cool stuff
But Christopher always declined. He said he liked being up on the roof
It was his favourite place
He liked hanging out with the pigeons, and being in the fresh air
I wasn't lonely anymore, because I had someone to play with
Dad didn't believe me, when I told him about Christopher.
I tried to tell him about my new friend, because I was worried about him
Every time I went up to the roof, Christopher was always standing on the ledge, looking down at the cars
I always ran to him, waited until he climbed down to the roof again
He had his sad days, sometimes he didn't want to play or hang out with me
We would sit silently together.
On those days, I worried that he might jump
I thought maybe Dad should go and talk to his father.
Instead, Dad went to the landlord and talked to *her*
She told him that he was the only tenant in the building with a child
None of the neighbours he spoke to had ever heard or seen a kid that looked like Christopher in the building
He said I shouldn't lie to him about big stuff like that.
I could get into serious trouble, saying that someone was trying to commit suicide on the premises
He said he figured I was acting out, because I was angry that we'd moved.
Even when I tried to take him up to the roof to introduce him to Christopher, Dad refused.
Dad told me he was much too busy to care about an imaginary friend
And Mom was always busy. She didn't want to hear about Christopher, either.
And so I knew that none of the grown-ups were going to care about helping him.

I was Christopher's only friend.
In September, school started.
I met other kids in the neighbourhood, kids my age
And when that happened, I didn't have as much time to spend with Christopher
But every day, I would go up to the roof, even if it was only for a few minutes
He liked helping me with my homework. Christopher was really smart.
And we still played games, still people-watched
He knew all the star constellations
Some nights, I took my blanket up to the roof, and a thermos of hot chocolate
We'd stay up there until it was too cold
Then I'd go back down to my room. I had to sneak out, because Dad thought that the roof was unsafe
One night, it snowed.
It was a week before Halloween, and it was the first snowfall of the year
I was really excited, as I watched the snow fall heavily from my bedroom window
It was thick, heavy flakes that looked like it wasn't going to stop for a long time
The sky was deep grey, with a beautiful pinkish tinge
I couldn't really sleep. I was too excited – especially since school had been cancelled the next day.
I loved snow days, wanted to make the most of my free day.
Early that morning, I snuck up to the roof
I wanted to know if Christopher was up there yet.
I wanted to talk to him,
And I wanted to see how the city looked shrouded in snow
I had to shove the heavy door open, pushing against it with my shoulder because of the heavy snow
"Christopher?" I called out.

He was standing on the ledge, just like always
Arms outstretched, eyes closed
I trudged through the thick snow, and went over to talk to him
We talked awhile, watching the snowplows clearing the roads
It was early, around six in the morning
The snow had mostly stopped, reduced only to a few flurries
The few cars on the road slid comically around on the patches of black ice, trying to keep control
Sidewalks were icy, unsalted
I asked Christopher if he would help me build a snowman
The snow was thick and fluffy, the perfect texture
We began rolling the snowballs. Christopher began forming the large base first.
I worked on the smaller snowball – the snowman's midsection
At one point, I glanced over to him, and froze
Christopher was trudging through the snow a few feet from me
He was smiling, his sweatshirt sleeves drawn over his hands to keep them warm from the wet snow
His sneakers made light crunching noises on the fresh snow, but he made no marks.
"Christopher, how are you not making any footprints?" I asked, surprised.
He stopped rolling the snowball, and raised his eyebrows at me
He stayed silent.
"Christopher?" I asked, confused.
How could he not make any footprints? The snow was so thick.
I was much lighter than him, and my boots sunk into the snow, creating small indents
"I never make footprints."
"Are y-you *dead*?" I asked, shaking the snow off my mittens. "Are you a *ghost*?"
Christopher shrugged. "Yeah."

I hoped he was joking. One look at his face, and I knew that he was deadly serious.

"Why didn't you tell me?"

"I thought you *knew*."

I frowned.

All this time, I had had no idea my best friend was a ghost!

I thought back to all the times we played together

I'd only ever hung out with him on the roof, never at his apartment – or mine.

Nobody else had ever seen him. Not my dad, or the landlord – not even the other neighbours.

We never took the bus down to the park, or went to the corner store for ice cream even when it was super hot out

And every time I was with him, he was always wearing the same thing – black sweatshirt, jeans, and purple sneakers

Even on the colder days, even on a snowy day such as that, Christopher was still wearing the same clothes

"How long have you been dead?" I asked, suddenly filled with sadness.

Had he been dead the entire time I knew him?

Or had he jumped at some point over the past few months since we'd met?

I didn't know.

"Years ago – way before I met you." Christopher gave me a sad look. "I've been dead for years, Eden."

All this time, I thought I had known him.

He was like the older brother I had always wanted

We got along quite well

But why couldn't he have told me something like this? This was *big*.

"You were dead all this time?" I asked, heartbroken. "Oh, Christopher, that's awful!"

The snowman sat forgotten, half-formed between us.

Christopher gave me a sad sort of look

"That's where I jumped," Christopher said, pointing at the ledge where he always stood. "It was a long time ago."
I went over to him, wrapped my arms around him – just like I had done countless of times before
The thought of him jumping to his death like that disturbed me to no end. I didn't want to think of him broken on the ground.
I wanted him to be alive and well
He felt real, solid
He told me that every day, he found himself up on the roof
It was like his last day on earth was on permanent reset mode – always starting the same way.
Him, on the ledge.
He was forced to relive his last moments for eternity
And every day, he jumped to his death.
That is, until he had met me.
When I had first come up to the roof, it was the first time he had been able to step off the ledge back onto the roof since his death.
It happened every day that I went up to the roof to spend time with him
When I was there, I made him feel happy, normal
I was able to distract him, keep his dark thoughts at bay
I was like his protector, a guardian of sorts
After he finally told me everything, I made extra sure to visit Christopher on the roof daily
I didn't want him to have to experience his death ever again.
Years later, I graduated from high school, and my parents retired
I had a choice to make – stay, or leave for University
I decided to stay.
I could do my schooling online, work from home.
I took on my parent's lease, stayed in the apartment
I didn't want to leave Christopher, knowing what he would go through every day
He had divulged to me some of what he'd been through before his death

I knew some of the trauma that he'd endured, and what led to that terrible decision to jump.

Every day, I went up to the roof, and hung out with Christopher

When I was in my mid-twenties, I had a son

I named him Johnathan Christopher – after my father, and my best friend

And every day, I brought little JC up to the roof with me to spend time with our resident ghost

GRACEFUL DANCER

She moves with such grace
Arm outstretched high above her head, hand delicate and elegant
She spins so fast, almost inhumanely fast
Around and around, like a spinning top
She lifts up onto her ball of her feet, easily supporting her weight
Stretching higher, touching the sky
And then, she is up on her pointe shoes
Balanced precariously on her toes
It is such a sight to behold
The dancer stretches out her long, muscled leg
She bows her arms, and dips low to the ground

Years of training have given her the lithe figure perfect for dance, with toned calves and thighs, feet arched
She lifts her leg up to her head, limbs flexible
She dances effortlessly, like no one is watching
Up on stage, performing for large crowds – and in the studio, practising at the barre
She stretches, body elongated
I watch her as she dances up on stage, the hardwood floor creaking underneath her pointe shoes
She wears white tights, and her black bodysuit
Her hair is in a tight bun, high up on her head
Tulle tutu in bright blue
I could watch her dance all day

TREES AT NIGHT

It is evening
I walk along the leaf-strewn grass, looking up at the orange sunset glow filter through the trees
It is a quiet, calm night.
Neighbours sit on their front porches, drinking beers, and cooking burgers on the grill
Summer is over, Autumn thrust upon us
Soon, the air will have winter's bite – the promise of snow
This is the perfect weather right now.
Slightly chilly at night, the dew settling on the long grass like diamonds
The woods are beautiful at sunset
The orange light filters through the veiny leaves, hitting them just perfectly
When it's about to rain, the leaves move in the wind, rustling as they turn

And when the sun finally sets, the beech trees glow a vibrant purple, and
blue
Shadowed in deep, rich hues
I like the solitude, the stillness
All my best thoughts come at night, when I am able to think without
daylight's distractions
I am my most creative at night, when the moon is high in the sky
It is when most everyone is asleep.